WINTER QUARTERS

PETER SCUPHAM

Winter Quarters

Oxford   New York

OXFORD UNIVERSITY PRESS

1983

Oxford University Press, Walton Street, Oxford OX2 6DP

London Glasgow New York Toronto
Delhi Bombay Calcutta Madras Karachi
Kuala Lumpur Singapore Hong Kong Tokyo
Nairobi Dar es Salaam Cape Town
Melbourne Auckland
and associates in
Beirut Berlin Ibadan Mexico City Nicosia

British Library Cataloguing in Publication Data

Scupham, Peter
Winter quarters.
I. Title
821'.914   PR6069.C9
ISBN 0-19-211957-5

Library of Congress Cataloging in Publication Data

Scupham, Peter.
Winter quarters.
1. War poetry, English. I. Title.
PR6069.C5544W5 1983   821'.914   83-4233
ISBN 0-19-211957-5

Set by Promenade Graphics Ltd.
Printed in Great Britain by
J. W. Arrowsmith Ltd., Bristol

Contents

Acknowledgements

Some of these poems first appeared in *Encounter, Here Now, PN Review, Poetry Wales, The Literary Review, The Present Tense* and *The Times Literary Supplement*, or were broadcast on 'Poetry Now' (BBC 2). The sequences *The Christmas Tree: 1944* and *Transformation Scenes* were first published by The Mandeville Press and The Red Gull Press respectively.

The Spanish Train

The little Spanish train curls in the hand,
Its coat of many colours; the June garden
Will blow to seed, find new snows and sierras.
Somewhere, beyond the phlox, the cherry wall,
Goya etches: tristes presentimientos,
And though his rooms are hung with all misfortune
The train draws down a truthful patch of sunlight,
A radiance not yet underpinned by shade
Or lost in the earth-closets of the garden:
Neither the last mile to Huesca taken,
Nor the fixed siren set upon the Stuka.

Now, on a sofa, the child holds a word:
Spain, where the rain goes, and a wooden train
Quite serious in its unclouded paintwork,
Its yellow bright as any Star of David.
While the small fingers look inside a carriage
Or hook and eye the polished dolly-wagons
The flowers prepare their faces for the night.
Shutters and bolts are drawn. There are long journeys
Which must be made. No saben el camino.
There is no remedy. There is no time.
The little Spanish train curls in the hand.

The Christmas Tree: 1944

I

Complements of the season,
  Fire, Fleet and Candlelight,
A curtain-work of velvet,
  The web and pin of night.

Out in the grey garden,
  The paths go nowhere at all,
A fruitless net of branches
  Holds to the frosted wall.

It is cold wood and silence,
  Unshapes of flint and loam,
Ground weathered into absence,
  And the bright sap called home.

The New Year brings a stranger,
  His shadow stains the land;
He waits upon your threshold,
  A live coal in his hand.

Against his throbbing advent,
  Flarepath and Bombers' Moon,
The sweet must of the fir-tree,
  The branches thick with rune.

Your roots are cut and broken,
  Your star is finger-high;
The mast-tree plumbs the centre,
  Its tinsel splits the sky.

2

There the brocades, woven against the darkness,
Quiet bevels of glass and figured walnut
Making their change of substance into reflection,

Calling the child, who, propped against his pillow,
Presses his eyes till they swell against the knuckle
And stares from his bed into the swarming pitch,

Alert for the jewels pinned on processional air,
Trinkets of light, a more than royal progress,
The unlocked treasuries of a ghost-kingdom.

The child slips down to the room where nobody comes,
Lured by a siren tongue to a virgin country
Where every contour is a familiar strangeness.

There are the robes hung over black-ice windows,
The tree which has decked itself, and sings to itself,
Blossoming there, O rich Arabian tree,

The Phoenix tree, rising each year from the ashes,
Freighted with ice and flame in a twist of glass,
Whose delicate birds are the birds of so, and no other,

Whose flowers and fruit are sufficient, sufficient still
For the child who stands, caught in the wavering crystals
Which foretell all: his image diminished, untarnished.

3

The life caught in its branches
   Crumbles in drying air,
A shiver of dark needles
   And a year stripped bare,

As cold as a clean bed-sheet,
   The stubbed wings in the sky,
The ache of an old floorboard
   Or the snow's white lie.

'Give me back my legions,'
   Cry Emperor and Child,
'That box of pretty soldiers
   Whose bones lie far and wild.'

Long miles of sighing forest
   Reach out, out and away;
Break ice on a birdbath,
   Scatter the crusts, and pray.

Dusk, and the twisting candles
   Blend shade and flying shade,
The quick and the dead link fingers,
   Their circle made, unmade.

The box is packed, my children,
   Gone where the dust-motes go;
Under a crease of tissue
   The softened colours flow.

Pathfinder

Night-riders gather, and all skies look east.
The stars are steady in their tight formations,
Crossing with light this grind of troubled air.
The house is softening its velvet textures,
Buoyed to its moorings by a bombers' moon.
Its charts record only the stretch of wood
Which gives, misgives, at the sleep-walker's touch,
And stranger-faces turn from watery mirrors.
Outside, the beaten grass is lost and grey
Where levelled meadows launch their thunders out,
Over the shining waters into Europe.
Working for shapes of life under closed lids,
The house is dreaming little flocks of questions:
Fidgets of dark glass tripping in the frame,
Easings of tread and riser at the stair.
The cows at dusk spoke only country matters
As daylight sank behind the window-bars,
And no pathfinder drops his marker-flares
Upon this crouching city of bad dreams.
Over the leaded grate, farmer and dog
Exchange their painted sentiments of loss
As the old home comes underneath the hammer.
The night dies on till all the tides are turned,
And though the ebb was deeper than the full,
From this, our common ground, we cannot single
That diminution in the homing waves
Which speaks of tears, which speaks of tears and flame.

Nights Turning In

Nights turning in, fold upon awkward fold,
Leaves of a burnt book whose dull pages crumble
Their brittle edges and discolorations.
The stitching weakens; flesh and spirit split.
Black epiphanies: a spring of night-sweats,
A text of dreams, a dance of matchstick bones
And soundless windows opening on no-place.
The hour-glass nips my sand against its fall.

Somewhere, across a street, a woman dies.
The knowledge drugs all childhood into sickness
And curtains flap out sharply at the bedside.
Nothing, nothing. A boy's head turns about
And elm-tops thresh across the greying light.
Cold bowls of spew: the shake, the severance
When something old and wrinkled can be still.
Love hovers there upon the slipping years.

Commotions of the dark, the soldier's time.
A faceless private twists against the wall,
Coughing small blood. A stretcher, swing of doors.
The neutered smells parade these corridors
And night softens a bruise upon each corner.
My sentry paces with his greatcoat stiff;
I take a prisoner to the sour latrine.
His grin shines there like a clutch of handcuffs.

Old bombers throbbing in, the gunfire tumbling.
Between this wake and sleep my sister sings
'A Bobsa sat in a little box bed,
And this is what the Bobsa said':
The winds blow hard through all your bricks and mortar,
They carry harm, though harm makes long delay,
Settling its spores against a full fruition.
The horseshoe at your door spills out its luck.

Conscriptions
National Service '52–'54

1. Cleanliness

Is the one song of our innocence.
We have become that which it is next to:
Every mess-tin has a silver lining
And greatcoats mint pure bobbles of fools' gold.
Is not the sun a high armorial fire
Which angels burnish into excellence?
Down the long barrack-room our bedding-cakes
Repeat their candy icing and grey fur.
Beauty lies one skin deeper. Look, the broom
Is pared and pared again to spectral white;
The bucket is, no doubt, intangible,
Whose cusp is moulded from the freezing air.
We have ascended Plato's giant ladder,
Worked our eyes free from sensual mote or beam.
Each cants a virgin rifle to the light,
Whose shining gyre repels the wanton dust;
The ghost of a flea would not escape our scrutiny.
We dream of purity: a myth of coal
Whitewashed to some immaculate Everest,
The world's grass trimmed into a uniform
By scissors neat and crisp as a wren's claw . . .

'Take his name, Sergeant, and dismiss.'

2. *Scapegoat*

Who are you there, huddled on your bed,
The sum and cipher of the awkward squad,
Your unbulled boots as round as innocence?
Nothing about you that will take a shine:
A soggy face, whose creases will not harden
To stiffening rubs of soap or these hot irons.
Unserviceable one, we circle round you,
Trimming our tackle to the Spartan code
And licking the parade-ground into shape.
Your fingers are all thumbs, your two left feet
Are mazy as your tangle of dull webbing.
Our silence covers up for you, our hands
Work your fatigues to parodies of order.
The small Lance-Corporal stares you cold and white;
His fingers itch to knock the silly smile
Off that dim face. You are our crying need,
The dregs and lees of our incompetence,
A dark offence, a blur on the sharp air.
These squares will not assimilate you now,
Whose discharge, something less than honourable,
Leaves our hutment stripped of all reminders
That something in the world could be in love
With pliant, suffering things that come and go.

3. *The Square*
(*Blackdown Camp*)

Can you draw from cold spring air
That whispering host which hovers lightly
Over the strutting heads of our brief Stentors,
Who rasp and wail with bulled and brazen throats,
Bothering our confusions into order?
Here the old regiments were brought to heel,
Dressed, and dismissed into the common clay.
Rosenberg knew it: nineteen-sixteen.
'Slow, rigid is this masquerade',
And the May Queen out of all her finery.
Something passes for sunlight on the Square,
And fading away in combes of Hampshire sand
Guard-room verandahs twist their Indian tricks.
Tongues fade, cross-fade; the air is empty,
Drilled hollow by the legions of the damned
That in the crossway and the flood had burial.
We are the soldiery of the nursery-floor,
The rasp of khaki coarse at neck and thigh,
Our heads held high by plasticine and matchsticks;
Who grow in grace, perfecting symmetries,
Learning to stand at ease upon the carpet,
Ready for Floor Games, and the Little Wars.

4. *Sunday*

A choleric sun, nailed to its meridian,
Bothers the lazy hours from slipping westward,
Idle on their afternoon parade.

These are the lone and level sands of time.
Asphalt, the old sweat, glisters a mirage;
Angled shadows drawl and dawdle.

Slow, slow, the reined-in coursers of the day:
A nest of lorries, fender snug to fender,
Bounces the aching light from glass to metal.

We yawn our backs upon the iron bedsteads,
Cupping our hands to cradle shaven heads.
Eyes hold nothing of the sky in them.

Someone writes the world a long, slow letter
Which will be sealed with a loving kiss.
A twisted tune breaks like a bad-luck mirror.

Unhappy pin-ups freeze in their chaste lockers;
Barrack the green shade with their secret curves.
Bad minutes drift their ciphers into years.

5. *Range*

'Your weapons are given you to kill the enemy.'
Corner him in your eye; his name is legion,
Or Boredom, or the Sergeant-Cook.
He jumps like a grasshopper from the breech,
Tinkles among the pebbles of the range
And dies there in a little spill of brass.
As sights are notched up, he appears again
Under the zoomorphic guise of Bull or Magpie,
Travelling by Inner and by Outer Circles.
We splay our aching legs, shoulder the kick,
And ask again for a report of him;
Riddled, he returns a dusty answer.
Don Quixote leans there at our shoulder:
Gestures and angles underneath his whiskers,
A furious windmill of small arms and cane.
There, where the flapping tic-tac of the Butts
Confuses hand and eye; there, there his tricks
Appear and disappear in shreds of cardboard.
This is your enemy: the aching sun,
That baulk of sand, the estuary's blue sky.
He is the slipping knot of bedclothes
Whose linen face collapses at your feet,
The man of straw, pierced by your pigmy lance,
Who dies his death: a thousand thousand cuts,
To bob and come, to bob and come again.

6. *Night Exercise*

From Inferno's lesser circles,
  Imps of darkness, sooterkins,
Crack their cloven hooves to sparkle,
  Barking at each other's shins.

Chilly fingers knuckle over
  Till the skin's as blue as woad:
Pin-up moon's a lonely lover,
  All the signals are in code.

Stars loose off their ammunition:
  Rounds of blank. Our comic turn
Leaps from its jump-off position,
  Frights the butter from the quern.

In a burst of Chinese crackers
  Fools make circles to Ducdame;
Walking dead go to the knackers,
  Hamlet's father doffs his armour.

Disrespectful groundlings grumble,
  From their traps the devils rise;
Thunderflash and thundergrumble
  Rub the sleepymen from eyes.

We are midnight's mischief-makers,
  Dreamers dithering their dreams:
Sectaries of quakers, shakers,
  Mice agley in best-laid schemes,

Lambs gone ravenous for slaughter –
  I kill you and you kill me;
Tell the Colonel's dirty daughter
  'Twas a famous victory.

7. *Assault Course*

Tarzan is swinging, all his ululations
On undulant display, but Jane is waiting
Somewhere in Italy: I trust and love you.
We flounder after him up scrawls of netting,
Tricksy reticulated interstices
Which catch a shoal of twitching fins and fingers.
Our pendulums of flesh on rope lianas
Soar like Lieutenant Robin and his Batman;
Piranhas, non-commissioned, coast the waters,
Apt for our boning and our filleting.
These are sad tracts of sand to founder in:
Limpopos set about with fever-trees,
Free-standing cliffs of absent-minded wall
And a Cloaca Maxima to drain us.
We sink with Carver Doone to the abyss,
Tipple with Moriarty to the Falls,
One with all those who lost their feet, and fell,
Whirling their cloaks about the Eiffel Tower
Or joking as they passed the nineteenth storey.
These are the ups and downs of exaltation,
Small dodgems of the flesh. We dive through tyres:
Hoops of old fire to set the tigers blazing,
And under catacombs of rolling canvas
Shake hands with Alan Quatermain, Tom Sawyer.
Through, over, under, off – a stocking stitch:
There's no doubt left that we must pull our socks up.

8. *Guard-Room*

The New Guard forms, is present and correct,
Stamping its dolly boots, slapping its rifles.
We dress according to the ancient lights.

I am their Corporal; at my conscription
They take their stint of turn and turn about,
Conjuring for me their forgotten faces.

Lights out in barrack-blocks: Alma, Dettingen.
The sky has moved into its winter quarters
Over this coarse plain, bruising to the heel.

The sentry's breath disperses a still plume.
We have dismissed the sun to his great arc;
The pendulum moves deep and slow beneath us.

Should some goodfellow come to bless this house,
He must be challenged, were it the Prince himself.
Even our shadows have offended us.

My lubber-fiends deploy and stretch their arms
To the one bar of our electric fire
Whose raw scrape intensifies the cold.

The Guard-room mirror plays its monkey tricks
And small hours crawl towards the edge of light,
A sticky silt brimming our mouths and eyes.

We are the tutelars, our field-dew consecrate,
A smear of cigarette-ash on the floor.
Even this dull ground needs a libation:

This staging-post for Somme and Passchendaele.
The Square whitens towards our armistice;
In France, their markers steady the parade.

9. *Sentries*

The inspection of shadows is our trade;
It is a business like any other.
Their stony faces are their misfortune:
Scratches of chalk on streaky blackboards.
When they speak, they do not raise their voices
And their complaints are blear and frivolous.
We know the fret and chafe of swinging iron,
The high wind slipping through a stretch of wire,
And little devils twirling in the dust
Abouts and roundabouts of wrinkled leaves.
Underneath the lamplight, the barrack-gate
Admits an air of cold authority,
Winking at our buttons, flickering ice
On swollen toecaps, lustrous ebonies.
We stamp their seal into a crush of gravel.
Let it all pass: ay, that's the eftest way.
We would rather sleep than talk;
We know what belongs to a watch.
Our relief is at hand; he will undertake it.
Wrapped in our winter pelt of pleated greatcoats
We fall into the consequence of dreams,
Careless who goes there, borrowing the night,
And will not stay to be identified.

10. *Prisoner*

You have fallen through it all: a cipher
Among the ranks you are reduced to,
The untamed residue of our glittering bull.
I watch your cropped skull bob between two Redcaps,
Those fresh-faced bullocks of our *Staatspolizei*
Stiff in their creases and their icy blanco.
We shall survive, but you are the survivor,
With nothing left to lose, or do, but time.
Your conduct prejudicial; crimed, impenitent,
Inured to having all the books thrown at you,
You do a Buster from the sliding train
Or slip your skin between the gated walls.
Your number's up in all the Standing Orders;
Our colours cannot call you. Your presence here
Is merely another absence without leave.

I link our wrists, trapping the bracelets on.
How shall we celebrate our Silver Wedding?
You flick a grin, strip with a knowing eye
My poor sleeves bare of sundry birdshit chevrons.
Oh, thing of darkness I acknowledge mine
By the conscription of a signature,
Your lightest word is ponderous to me,
But I will take you for the night's duration
While Moon ticks off the hours on her demob chart.
We shall walk out together, much in love,
For such a petty pace as you would creep to,
And hunt the shadows with a pack of lies,
Fusing the blue ghosts of our cigarettes
Till sleep takes you, and a sallow lamplight
Bones your neat head to cunning innocence.

11. *The Tents*

The tents brown out a Scottish hillside:
A canvas of cold water drenching down
From all the tops into the lagging valley.
We drape our beds and rust like iron things.
I would not know that soldier's face again:
Merely a wedge, a pallor from which talk
Breaks out and runs in darker rivulets,
Working its horrid nonsense into corners.
Night after night he picks a sentence over
Until we riddle out the half-told secret.
His fingers are the draw-strings to a knife
Which keens and wakes with him beside the pillow.
He swears that it will get them, do them in;
The knife knows better as it sleeks a blade
Which never will let blood, or cut the knot
That tied his brother's neck to breaking-point
At the fixed, formal hour. That guilt must be,
Can only be, a blinding innocence.
His twitching face settles against the dark;
Rain courses down, icing the cold cheeks,
Fretting its runnels deep into the clay.
What kindness in the world loads him with this:
An amulet to cut and come again,
Peeling the running air to slips of light
And tender for the dead, surrendered flesh?

12. *Envoi*

There lies your way, Major,
   A year of the old parade
Before the ribboned tunic
   Must gather dust and fade

As the hung smoke of battles
   Fought in the long-ago,
Memories of sap and salient,
   Tobruk or Anzio.

Now, our final parting,
   Neat, dry as your hair.
(The newest batch is wheeling
   Over the sun-struck Square.)

'Yes, sir. Demob tomorrow.
   No, sir. University.'
'Missed all that. Never made it –'
   (Staff College, Camberley.)

Somebody else in the morning
   To serve, to stand, to wait,
To type Battalion Orders,
   To keep the long files straight.

'Too long in the tooth, Corporal.
   Shake hands. Good luck to you.'
'Thank you, sir. Are you sure that . . . ?'
   'No . . . Nothing else to do.'

Farewell to all our greatness,
   To musket, fife and drum,
Before the new lean armies,
   The new lean missiles come.

Samuel Palmer: The Bellman

I

So many loves and passions in the dust:
The city black and swollen, a bad dream
Shaping the night to its own lumps and savours.

Its river–voices will not come to rest
Nor its tumultous brew of humours clarify,
Though keys to courts and tenements rust bare.

Tongues run blind far out into these reaches;
Days are laid waste by this trafficking.
The moon rising tells another story

To Samuel and his nurse, there at the window.
Its metals blend in the ascendant;
The garden fills with smokes of dusty silver.

An elm crosses its shadows on the wall;
The motion of its growth is held, opposed.
A plying web gathers its strength about them.

The two of them share Milton's words with us:
'Vain man, the vision of a moment made,
Dream of a dream, and shadow of a shade.'

'Seclusion without desolateness', he wrote,
'And darkness without horror'. In this place
To which his working hand and eye have led us
      We are made freemen.

Ancient, you renew the hills and valleys;
They will confide the secrets of their dancing.
Your inks have run into a spire of smoke,
      The houses' foliage.

Old England is a pile of matted shadows,
A plaid of deep grass; where the meadows draw
The little threads far out into confusion
      Our footsteps follow.

Your hatchings cross and thicken: falling ground,
Breastwork of thatch and clay, a brush of leaves
Where all the sharp, sweet voices of the day
      Hunch in their feathers.

The rising moon describes her magic circle;
Mushrooms pry blind among the pricking dew.
The Bellman's chime gutters our lights away
      From country matters.

We rest in darkness, darkness which has come
Out of the grave to tell us that the dead
Are undivided, and their absent breaths
      Are fruitful for us.

La Primavera

In this, her kingdom, fictions of light gather,
Suffusing the pale flesh in a grave trance
Which is her thought, and whose desires are other;
The light airs hover over a ring dance.
The grace-notes hold there, and the hung fruits glow:
The riders all are fallen at San Romano.

The garden shaped my steps to her consent;
I read the text of her inviting hand,
Knew time to be dissolved, the censors absent.
No city shook its bell-notes on the land,
No New Jerusalem: mere trembled gauze
Whose veils disclosed and hid the garden's laws.

Then, when I turned, light lived from edge to edge
And each defining line became the source.
The glancing room conferred a privilege
To enter silence, follow out its course,
Turn to a window and exchange a stare
With frost laid cold on paths: untrodden, bare.

I knew this light, those breaths our dead resign,
That gift of tongues which holds authority,
Those dancers on some gold horizon-line,
That chosen ground. Her kingdom set me free
To share an hour unmeasured by the clock,
A space drawn freely between key and lock.

How, though, to judge and weigh the shift of planes
Or tell the climbing foreground from the sky?
Under the music come the dragging chains
And we are littered under Mercury.
Arrows must fledge the Saint; the pearl flesh dulls,
And Mary weeps there in the Field of Skulls.

La Derelitta bows her head, life thrown
To one eternal gesture of despair:
The flawless courses on unyielding stone
Pave the twinned elements of earth and air.
Savonarola burns; the scorched tears run,
Time throws a black smoke up against the sun.

Yet the globes hang there, and the star-flowers spill,
Speak mortal names on an immortal ground
Which is the ground of being, printless still;
The grove still sighs with music beyond sound.
Hortus Inclusus, and there is no stir
From haloed leaf and tree announcing her.

Transformation Scenes

1. *Evening in the Park*

The groundwork fading, shadow crossed on shade,
   A no-man's-land of cold uncertainty:
The crooked sunlight breaking up the glade
   And something ciphering from tree to tree.
      Low tides of night-dressed wings,
      Flickers and pesterings,
Enhance the opiate of ruins ruinous,
   The burst of star-shell fallen to the floor,
   The spectral ravens croaking 'Nevermore'
      In tones most ominous.

Back at the Hall, red drugget leads the maze:
   A ghostly peepshow of embroidered rooms.
Though sometime bones of little good-dog Trays
   Whiten the wet mould of their chamber-tombs,
      Each stuccoed altitude
      Gold-frames a buxom nude –
But all the garden gods have smudged into the rain.
   Such absent-minded tritons in the lake!
   We wait, and feel again the long light shake,
      But will not come again

To tease the trinkets from the jewel-box,
   The baubles from a Georgian Christmas-tree:
The must and rust of humming-birds and clocks,
   The filigree, the tat, the pedigree.
      Time now to stump the hill
      Where stone is dressed to kill
With bobbled obelisk and dumpy octagon,
   Where some sly toad lifts an unjewelled head,
   Revisiting the mansions of the dead,
      Each son et lumière gone

Which might, perhaps, throw a bewitching light
  On these dishevelled fictions of an age
Diminishing, kaleidoscopic, bright,
  A minuet on a revolving stage.
        It is the moon's affair.
        Her blue blood washes where
The frost of cardboard castles thaws into the grass,
  Small pyramids tell tales of smaller kings.
  Oh, button mushrooms in your fairy rings,
        Tout passe, tout casse, tout lasse.

2. *Scott's Grotto, Ware*

'From noon's fierce glare, perhaps, he pleased retires
Indulging musings which the place inspires.'
So, Scott of Amwell, fearful of the pox,
    Shifted his garden ground;
Quarried his Quaker frissons from the rocks
Till winking, blinking, Dr Johnson found
A Fairy Hall, no inspissated gloom.

But slag and pebble-bands decay and fall,
The glimmerings and lustres fly the wall
Whose rubble freezes to a dull cascade.
    The flint-work strikes no spark
And its begetter dwindles to a shade
Composing, decomposing in the dark,
Scribbling an Eclogue in a candled room,

Turning from Turnpikes or Parochial Poor
To the close circuits of this tilting floor,
Caves editing a Gentleman's Magazine
    Of cold and fading shells
Eased from their chambers of pacific green
To ride the beaches and the long sea-swells,
Then pressed into this ragged, alien womb

Which closes its dark backward and abyss,
Its miniature, yet Stygian emphasis
Upon your childhood voice, its terrors crossed
    Upon their own reply.
'Oh, if you're lost, then tell me *where* you're lost,
I'll kiss away the little deaths you die
And bring a light to raise you from the tomb.'

3. *Ornamental Hermits*

Veiled melancholy, mid-day accidie,
   Improvings of the landskip sheathed in rain:
We dwell, not live, shifting from knee to knee
   In robes as uncanonical as plain,
Nodding, like Homer, over knucklebones,
   (Cold vertebrae a starwork on the floor)
Serviced by birdsong: vespers, compline, nones –
   The cycles of unalterable law.
Our eremitic dirt, our nails prepare
   A mortifaction close to Godliness;
Under the tangled prayer-mats of our hair
   Each sours into his mimic wilderness.

The desert fathers, locked into each cell,
   Knew all the pleasures that retirements bring:
The succubus, the tumbling insect-hell,
   Assault of breast and thorax, thigh and wing.
Our bark-house windows, open to the sky,
   Show vellum faces, blind-stamped and antique:
A glaze of rigor mortis at the eye,
   A tear-drop crocodiled upon the cheek.
The unread Testament aslant each knee
   Will not dispel the simple moth and rust
Corrupting us, degree by slow degree,
   Into the scattered frictions of the dust.

We beck, we hoist our creaking arms, we nod,
   Blessing processionals of cane and fan,
Attuned to Paley and his tick-tock God
   Or swung in gimbals pre-Copernican.
And who dare call our observation vain?
   The celebration, not the celebrant
Will keep the ancient order clear and plain;
   We too are arks of His great covenant:
God's weathercocks, upon his axles pinned,
   The beads of an industrious rosary,
Tibetan prayer-wheels turning in the wind,
   Imprisoned things which float the bright dove free.

4. *Portmeirion*

A slatted nest of pastel boxes hides
  The unfrocked Emperor of Considered Trifles,
Who, from some frolic cubicle decides
  New dispositions for old sacks and rifles.
    Gardeners, with water-can and paint,
    Furbish each rose and plaster saint
      With fresh bravura.

Or have these cracked and speckled eggshells hatched
  The frippery Princes of High Cockalorum,
Preening themselves about the gimcrack, patched
  With paper marbling and a fine decorum.
    We courtiers swell a scene or two,
    Feather their nest, improve a view
      Stippled as Seurat.

So what's to do but pace and pace about,
  Wearing our motley, and our Welchman's hose?
There's something déshabillé in our rout;
  The Buddha's stomach flows and overflows.
    Alice won't play. Why has she come,
    All frumpishness and suck-a-thumb?
      The place can't lure her,

Though the gold-leaf is laid upon the green
  And night will see the uncomplaining air
Gauze out its pretty transformation-scene,
  Swish rockets leaping from the tiny Square –
    That way the Old King left the town,
    His ashen blessing powdered down –
      Such sprezzatura!

5. *The Makers*

The dinky castles slip into the sea,
Though primped in paper flags and button shells;
A deckle-edge of ocean lips and swells,
Mining and slighting all our quality.
        We see
Their looped and window'd raggedness decline
        Into a sift of sand,
Hardened and barred as wind and Eastern wave design.

The scarlet toadstools pack themselves away,
The Christmas Cakes are crumbling to the plate;
The royal icings of their blood and state
Are one with all the snows of yesterday.
        The tray
Still keeps the touch of sweetest marzipan,
        Though little tongues of flame
Nibble the tissues into which their colours ran.

Gardens and gaieties are blown to seed,
The nymphs are crying down their party frocks;
The peacock straggles back into his box,
The secateurs are rusting in the weed.
        Agreed,
The gnomons are in shade; each gnome's expression
        Feeling the rot set in,
Is weathered slowly to a deepening depression,

But Homo Joculator starts again.
Though dyed in sinks of great iniquity
His mackintosh is black for luck, and he
Is whistling as he potters in the rain,
        The pain
Absorbed by cupola and curlicue,
        Those inching distances,
Castles in Spain which lend enchantments to the view.

Or

To step out into the drying garden,
Or rest greenly under the swarming branches –
The question rests in its own equipoise
And blue weighs out its great indifference.
Droit de Seigneur: the springing sunlight,
Here, or upon the antique Malvern Hills,
Will choose Copernicus, and Ptolemy.

To turn the first page of the great unread,
Or idle down a long-familiar margin –
The fingers know direction as they move,
And we will take their curious attention
Closely to heart; observe the Brimstone's flight
Who must explore mansions of air and light,
For his crisp yellow is definitive.

To follow shadow's course along the hill,
Or lift the eyes to dazzles of plain sky –
We wake to ceremonial chorus, find
Each blade of grass resolving Hamlet's question:
An old cat, fuddled in the border dew,
These flowers, half-opened and appropriate.
On a May morning, the word is golden.

Possessions

(M. R. James)

Shy connoisseur of ogee, icon, rune,
  Professor Prufrock ruminates decay:
Old Crowns and Kingdoms, food for thought and worms,
  All preservations held beneath the moon,
All sleeping dogs which can be kept at bay
  By gloss and glossary of well-thumbed terms.
His monograph extends by one dull page –
The last enchantment of his middle-age.

A fugitive from groves of Academe,
  The salt groynes running black from sea and sky
Betray his buried life down miles of sand.
  Low-tide: the beach is ebbing into dream,
Cold bents and marram-grass hang out to dry
  On swollen dunes. Deep in the hinterland
The calf-bound pages fox in white-sashed Halls
And stonecrop tightens on the churchyard walls.

Oh, blackthorn, unassuming country wear,
  Oh, modest rooms booked in some neat hotel:
Such pleasantries of the quotidian
  Are crossed by a miasma in the air.
Though bridge, or golf, might make him sleep as well
  And better than thy stroke, why swell'st thou then?
Bell, book and candle fail: the shadows mesh;
He counts the dissolutions of his flesh,

Appalled by faces creased from linen-fold.
  His textual errors thicken into sin,
Sour skin and fur uncoil about the night,
  Grotesques are hatching from the burnished gold
And countless demons, dancing on a pin,
  Repeat *a real fright, a real fright* . . .
Brandy, the first train home. The past dies hard
In stench and flare of bed-sheets down the yard.

2
(*Walter de la Mare*)

Grave summer child, lift your unnerving eyes:
Black bird-beads, drinking at the fluid light.
Whatever sifts among the unread leaves,
You pick your way, no Jenny Wren so neat,
Through Brobdingnag, here where the old aunts traipse.
Billows of shade, each face so loose and vague:
The stuff and nonsense clinging at their lips
As dusty, musty, as an antique wig.

A Conversazione. Old affairs
Flutter in broken heartbeats to decay,
Their ribbons fading into family ties.
Only huge, grown-up clouds for passers-by,
Cooling slow images in Georgian panes
Which close on rosewood, darken up the glaze
Of Dresden, and that chandelier which leans
Weak lustres over unplayed ivories.

The daylight shutters down, the white moths climb,
The house aches into whisper and desire.
You lie in bed, prim as the candle-flame
Pressing against the wing-beats in the air,
While nodding flower-heads and scents grow pale,
Mist curls where willows clarify, or dim.
As murmurs thicken in the Servants' Hall,
The callers gather; you are not at home.

3
(Rudyard Kipling)

The skull's base burning, and a swelling pain.
  A migraine of the soul: the Gods withdraw
Who made their Headings plain, and plain again,
    Whose word was Duty, and who spelled it Law.
      All slips beyond his reach – in the dark wood
      Where a wild nonsense claws substantial good.

The Lord was not there when the House was built,
  Though strength lay in the Mason's grip, the Sign,
And some who knew lie out in France, the silt
    And regimental headstones hold the line.
      Air thick with sighs; dead children stretch their hands
      To the Wise Woman, she who understands.

Is this the end, is this the promised end?
  Strange voices travel by Marconi's wire;
The crooked cells proliferate and blend,
    The cut runs counter to the hand's desire.
      A high wind wraps in winding-sheets of rain
      His House of Desolation, closed on pain.

They work about him at the razor's edge,
  Coax the indifferent stars to purblind sense:
Green simples, grounded by an English hedge,
    A surgeon, wiser than his instruments.
      He is returned, in ignorance, from the Gates.
      Under the draining tides the Day's Work waits.

Fachwen: The Falls

Green upon green: the crag discloses
Oak leaves over coronals of fern;
In quick vernacular the Fall rises,
The field's tilt makes clear and plain

Its puzzle of gorse, rough cups of harebell,
Ling and heather bonded to the height,
Soft crosses of yellow tormentil
Fringing a crop of split slate.

These flowers of the high pasture,
Grazing colour from a chancy sky,
Swell stem to blossom, become other.
Time adds, and cancels out, another day.

Butterflies in a coarse garden
Twirl clarities of white and red;
Poise and fold, the life hidden
Under the brief stain of a shade.

And arms, crooked on a grass terrace,
Ease to fronds of the sun's fire,
Warm as longing, a kept promise,
Or cool, mortal and beyond desire,

While the loose bolts of polished water,
Letting their silks and satins down,
Preserve in tricks of light and amber
The seeming of a world of stone.

Innocence: a stud of more-than-pebbles
Under their late-summer pelts of moss –
The unlicked cubs, Pliny's bear-shapes
Fostered by boulders, cumbersome wet-nurses
Lurching about a chatterbox of water
And hung with tingling webs, each crack and hollow
A choke of mould, a nest of quick decay.

Passage: a pack-horse bridge, the dolmens crossed
On stretchers of cold iron, their flat maps
An iconography of nowhere, traverses
Where wood-ants tease and flicker out their angles
Over the spread and eddy of the Fall.

Decay: the broken body of the hill,
Sulking a bruise of green and violet shale
Over the gritstone and conglomerate,
Twisting a cottage beaten to its hearth,
A floor wafered with an absent roof.

Bedrock: the Quarry Hospital, which bares
A mortuary slab of dressed and guttered stone.

3

The animation and suspense of water,
Where swelling stones, which rolled and gathered moss,
Point their white flocks the error of their ways,
Steady the channels' cut and counter-cross;
Where spinning threads pay out about the maze
Of time before, of time to follow after.

Here, Gothic slime, coagulate and brown,
Hung stiff above the brabble and the foam,
And blocky boughs peeled off to the half-nude.
Matthias Grünewald at Isenheim:
The landscape struck into its attitude,
The melancholia of the North set down.

Above, blent green against a chalky blue
Whose fiction reaches to a distant star,
And branches levelling those fans across
Which carry space without a spill or jar.
The plunging light is held against the press
Yet slips a trifle of its substance through

To quiver on a needle-point of grass,
Sharpen a saw of bracken, patch a stone
Whose ghosts of lichen bleach into the air.
The films of shaky white are on the turn
Where foliage lays a shaft of hillside bare,
Narrows an eye through which the waters pass.

The mid-point view: an equipoise of shade
Clouding the oaks which crutch down to the lake,
The yaffle with a cry stuck in its throat,
The heart of water, at its fall and break –
A glass which fractures to its own clear note,
A bright thing lost among a darkening wood.

4

Spread shade rusting to mould, turns of a no-track
Pulled hard, and against the drive of the waters:
That sullen tone of a voice confused, Brythonic,
Void of sense – a fool's reply to a question
Long fleshed in the grounding of church and chapel.

Then a cut to the bone; now, the brief whip-flick
Of bramble or nettle, skin's hairline fractures
Which heal, as this heals not, though green disguises
The hill's hurt: that probing, dressing of gangers
Bargained into the grave as the rains rubbled
Waste and spoil to the lake and its grey deceptions:
Fish-tunnelled hills, quarries of blur and quaver . . .

Ling brightens. Somewhere off to the right-hand
Sun plays to an empty pit and gallery:
Gouges brimmed with half-light. Topping the incline,
A smashed hut, and a spool of snaking cable
Angling down its bait: a dead thing rising.
Riding light on the ridge, thickets of hazel
Speak of spent lungs reaching into the freshets;
Small things hover or dart, swim in a shoal of bracken . . .

The Fall scores the hillside a little deeper.
Waters of Life, of Babylon: cold, unfailing.

5

If you could read this Chinese charactery,
Ideograms of twig crossed in the plash,
Grasses which rune 'Wish you were here',
Or 'This is a dry house shared with midges',

Then we could make the landscape our device,
And spell messages, such as 'Yes, I am waiting
Under the mountains by the falling water',
Or 'I expect your letter with impatience'.

As the Provincial Governor has left town,
I, his clerk, must write his letters for him,
Juggling, with such Mandarin as is at my command,
Flowers and absence, seasons and expectation,

Noting the brilliance, versatility,
With which the waterfall adjusts its dress;
How screens diminish to a single thread
But seem to find no trouble in maintaining

A style beyond all doubt or criticism.
The grass, now that I look more closely,
Is what is lost in the translation,
But says, so far as I can follow it:

'We have here a true voice at last.
Minor, no doubt, but perfectly in key.
I think we can say water has found itself
And will now go on to break new ground.'

Such, perhaps, is the letter I shall send.
No doubt the Governor would have more to say
Than this, entrusted to a cockle boat
Of stanzas rigged a trifle carelessly.

After Ovid, Tristia

Deeper the drifts now, rain and sun won't ease
This crabbed and crusty land a north wind scours,
Each snowfall hard upon another's heels
And summer elbowed from the frozen year –
These Arctic gales brew up a special fury,
Whipping the tall towers down, whirling our roofs off.
We shivering men, in pelts and galligaskins,
Put no more than a bold face to the world:
Each hair's an icicle, a shaken tinkle,
And blanching frost makes all beards venerable.
Our wine becomes its jar, stone-cold and sober
It stands its round; we break our drinks off piecemeal.
More news? How rivers lie in manacles,
And how we quarry water from the lake?
Our feet trudge in the wake of summer boats;
Our horses' hooves ring hard against each wave-crest.
Over new trackways bridging secret currents
The Russian oxen tug their simple carts.

Kingfisher

December took us where the idling water
Rose in a ghost of smoke, its banks hard-thatched
With blanching reeds, the sun in a far quarter.

Short days had struck a bitter chain together
In links of blue and white so closely matched
They made an equipoise we called the weather.

There, the first snowfall grew to carapace,
The pulse beneath it beating slow and blind,
And every kind of absence marked the face

On which we walked as if we were not lost,
As if there was a something there to find
Beneath a sleep of branches grey with frost.

We smiled, and spoke small words which had no hold
Upon the darkness we had carried there,
Our bents and winter dead-things, wisps of cold.

And then, from wastes of stub and nothing came
The Kingfisher, whose instancy laid bare
His proof that ice and sapphire conjure flame.

Night Walk

We found night in her tower, lifting each veil
And stain of cloud; our space grew full and bare,
The midnight blue tempered to ash and haze.

There was a crush of light on seas of grass,
Two faces bitten by a Chinese moon
And Venus making play with her small mirror.

Cold was crouching, huddled into shadow
Where trees displayed their pearly barbs against us,
Staked at the taut rim of an aching lawn.

We learnt the skills of frost, moved in our absence,
Ghosting our thoughts upon that polished bone.
The clocks were struck into profound silence.

And as we walked, bruised on the rigid ground,
The blood was bitter ichor in our veins,
Though singing in its courses with the spheres.

Saturnalia

The steward robs the orchard,
Strips birdsong from the year;
Io Saturnalia,
And a great paunch of beer.

Merry Andrew, tall man,
Your face cold as the snow,
Maria, sweet vixen,
How does your garden grow?

What should you burn in winter?
The dry stuff of the heart.
Hung with a wicked tinsel
The boughs cut and part.

Clouding the horn lantern
Time goes by on the wind;
The flame shakes, is shaken,
The snow is left behind.

A cloth of cold canvas,
Breath molten on the air,
Marriage of shade and shadow,
And the Fool crouched there.

Ship of Fools

The spindrift took us, and a chancy blue
   Twisted our compass from the homeward tack.
No spirit moved upon the waste; each knew
   The chafe of motley salt upon his back.

There was no thought, in the dead reach of night,
   Our timbers pitched against a sure decline,
To find the water sliced with careless light,
   Our lean hold parcelled out with bread and wine.

Field Glasses

Clouded beyond repair,
Each lens, whose purple bloom
Once zeroed in on air
And filled the prismed room

With O's and eyes of light,
A shaken moon or flare
Which slid across the night
And left its absence there,

Or eased a rainbow bridge
Across the migrant dawn
To bird and foliage;
The magic circles drawn

Round planes, their vapours trailing,
A cricketer's white ghost,
The Admiral's plain sailing,
The first one past the post.

No wonder, brought to light,
The weight deceives the hand,
With life brought down in flight
And lost in no-man's-land.

The landscape filled and sealed:
The long horizon's round,
The visionary field,
A thicket of dead ground.

And each cold retina
Holds, as the victim's eye
The leaning murderer,
A scratched and swelling sky.

Notes from a War Diary

(H.J.B. 1918–19)

1. *Madelon*

This is the song the poilus sing,
    Madelon! Madelon! Madelon!
'Et chacun lui raconte une histoire,
    Une histoire à sa façon.'

A captured goat in the Canteen Car,
    Driven by 'Darky' Robinson,
Magpies, poppies and marguerites,
    Crosses are wreathed among the corn.

'Glorious weather all the time',
    (Shelling of Ablois St Martin),
To a walnut tree, by the Villa des Fleurs,
    Faux-Fresnay, Vaux, Courcemain.

He's never seen two prettier girls,
    With manners to match, pink dresses on,
Little Monique, Jacqueline,
    Mme Pinard – or is it Pinant?

And a stolen flight with Paul Scordel,
    (Back in time for parade at 9),
'Regardez à gauche pendant la spirale',
    (A mustard-yellow A.R. Type 1).

'La servante est jeune et gentille,
    Légère comme un papillon,
Comme son vin son œuil pétille,
    Nous l'appelons La Madelon.'

But seven die at the Aerodrome,
    (Spads, appareil de chasse, monoplane),
'Forget your sweethearts, forget your wives',
    A Bréguet dives on a Voisin.

'Adieu Champagne, Villa des Fleurs',
  To the Airmen and the waving corn,
The convoy leaves the little Square,
  Beaumont, St Omer and Hesdin.

'Hope for a revoir bientôt',
  Thirty-eight years, to the day, in June,
Back 'en passant' to the Villa des Fleurs,
  To Faux-Fresnay and Courcemain.

Canterbury bells in the garden still,
  The house closed up, the shutters on,
And Monique dead at twelve years old,
  And the walnut tree cut down and gone.

What was the song the poilus sang?
  Madelon! Madelon! Madelon!
'Et chacun lui raconte une histoire,
  Une histoire à sa façon.'

2. *Echoes*

Like him, a survivor,
  His notebook lays bare
The exact words cut
  On the Picardy air,

And vanished Commanders
  Are echoes, catcalls:
'Well, any answer to
  Captain P's "Balls".'

A parade-ground whispers,
  Under August sun,
Of deeds, decorations:
  'There's more to be won.'

From a field in the field:
  'Very gratifying to me.
I'm proud of you, and I want you
  To be proud of me.'

That intolerable, urgent
  Intent of the dead,
Now light as a high-summer
  Thistledown head,

As his own unheard voice,
  Lips shaping 'C'est bon',
With the wind in his ears
  In that A.R. Type 1.

3. *Armistice*

Epernay. Took lorry along Dormans road
Under shellfire, dodging shells for a joke.
For no purpose took 7 cars for a ride.

Supper with 'Flamande', Jeanne, et le petit chat.
Saw 2 dead Germans, one with skull blown off,
Lying in house, partially gnawed by rats.

Scene over lights with Sergeant-Major Ford.
Headquarters moved now to Valenciennes.
Remain, pro tem, reading 'Sylvestre Bonnard'.

No guns audible at night. Ceasefire?
With car on Arras road. Hindenburg Line.
'Rindfleisch Westphalien', dead gunners, wire.

Walk with Smethurst down by the canal.
Graves, Château gardens, pansies and 'last rose'.
M's birthday. Weather keeps rainy, dull.

Birthday parcel and letter arrive from home.
Felt seedy and weak. Many cases of flu.
Put panes and canvas windows in the tram.

Rain continues. Heard death of Corporal Gosse,
Heard 'Jock' Kemp, 18, died of 'Spanish' flu.
Heard German envoys arrived for armistice.

Gunflashes still visible at night.
Terrier 'Judy' foully done to death
By Cook. Canine attempt on 'Nan', the goat.

Noticed flags out at Escadoeures.
Told news of ARMISTICE at Scotch Canteen.
Kings in flight. Unloaded Canteen stores.

Cambrai Park. Statue to Blériot.
'L'homme est un puits où le ride toujours recommence.'
Contemplations, Victor Hugo.

Trouble with Lieutenant Alec. Under arrest
For setting bar up in the Troops' Canteen
And selling whisky meant for Sergeants' Mess.

Revert to Private at my own request.

4. *Convoy*

Fifty yards between the Sections,
    Epernay, Courcemain, Cambrai:
Soundless convoys grinding on to
    Hesdin, Abbeville, Beauvais.

Sleep in fallowland in grass,
    Sleep out under apple tree;
Vauxhall, Talbot, Thorneycroft,
    St Pol, Meaux and Couilly.

Six by six the Sections close
    To their five-yard interval,
August sun, and rubber molten,
    All remaining cars on call.

'Freddy' Williams, Holdaway,
    (Offensive on the Amiens Front),
'Jock' Kemp, 'Darky' Robinson,
    'Paddy' Lloyd and Corporal Hunt,

Keeping date and keeping distance,
    Flesh and metal paper-thin,
Fère, Laloge, Forêt de Crécy,
    Tyre-tracks lightly pencilled in.

Still the harmless shells dip over,
    Where long-gathered harvests wave;
Sergeant Major Ford is picking
    Flowers for his Corporal's grave.

5. *Fin*

Madelon is left behind,
Her dispersal papers signed.

Spasmodic progress, mile by mile,
'Feeling pretty seedy still.'

Mons, Cambrai, Valenciennes,
By moonlight through Poix, Amiens.

Train-raid. Sleeping officers
Relieved of whisky and cigars.

'Khaki baked, new underclothes,'
Bread and bully, jam and cheese.

'Walk to Obelisk. Fine View.'
See 'Yes Uncle': a Revue.

March from the Delousing Camp
With books, flint implements and lamp –

'A trial for me.' Full marching order,
Kit-bag slung upon the shoulder,

Columns of four, and keeping step
To the harbour at Dieppe.

Channel-crossing. Dull, mild night.
South Foreland and North Foreland light.

Wait for tender. Disembark.
Fenchurch Street from Tilbury Dock.

Thetford under snow: the buzz
Of twenty different offices,

Buns and chocolate and tea,
'The Padre's curiosity.'

Cambridge station. Home at 10,
Lift on Royal Mail Van.

Soldier, scholar, he arrives
To what is proper: 'great surprise',

And ends the tale he never told:
'Wake naturally. Stiff bronchial cold.'

The Cottages

This is a day for things that are not there,
    Or there as lightly as a water-skein
Which dwindles back into the summer air.
    Appearances are flitting once again,
And cottages which cobbled out a street
    Stumble to hammers rocking through and through,
Forcing the sky to patch what's incomplete
    With scraps of rain and cloud, and raggy blue.

The orders all are down, and what we own
    Slips from our fingers; time takes us in hand
And finds our reaching fingers slip to bone.
    It's bone and broken bone can understand
This smell of woodsmoke coarsening the air,
    The secret voices ghosted to desire,
The little semblances of life laid bare,
    The hives and combs flooded with light and fire.

Strange that the dead should carry so much weight,
    Their last corruptions come of moth and rust,
The street grown strange, and strangely intimate,
    Their footsteps rising on a stair of dust –
And on the common ground which props the scene
    A chimney pot takes root in moils of clay,
Curling a rim of soot, easing a green
    Out of the darker houses, the decay.

Incident Room

'Police. You haven't heard, then?'
A pause takes breath. 'There's been a body found.'

The two stand burly, gentle at the gate.
Here, bones clean over in a shifting ground
Where deep, medicinal roots are intertwined;
Thrushes leave picks of shell on the back sill.
Though days confuse and motive works awry
Leaves measure out some strength; the roses
Cluster forgivably, cerise against wet light.
The language of flowers is not all hidden from us.

'Down there, beyond your garden.
A woman. Some children found her.'

Our places. The Jungle, silky once with poppies,
Now run from seed into a greenstick scrub.
The Saddlery – gone: a nest of curling tack
Blind-stamped back into the limy mould.
Higher, the Sweet Little Garden: old haunt
For white-webbed blackberries barbed about the dew.
Solid with life, all seasons in accord –
Till the Contractors flayed it to the clay.

'No. Yesterday afternoon.
She could have been there since the weekend, though.'

We have our shrine: Genio Loci, a lay figure
Crouched and wrinkled in his niche of shells,
Weathering it out by his own calendar.
Our paths lead to his particulars;
His wave-soft pebbles offer us assurance.
Tutelary, but asleep; blind as the sunk pool.
The flower-heads cup for sun till evening
Draws down unsafely at our patchy fence.

'Slim, dark hair cut short.
Did you hear anything, anything at all?'

A net of sound is trawled about these rooms:
Carriage of clocks, the stray and fret of tongues,
A pearly mutter from the kitchen screen.
The collared doves complain about our weathers,
Footsteps, checked, trip the hill-path down
Or climb against the grain by dusky lamps.
Pain reached no threshold. In small discourtesies
Our brick and woodwork wear themselves away.

'There may be photographs.
They won't look very pleasant, I'm afraid.'

The house labours under our care, our love.
The speechless books and unframed music fail
As in the garden strangers pause and stare
At the vague underworld of grass and stone.
The glass drifts out of focus; bounds are beaten
Where the wild wood and the wild world make one,
And all is absence, absence without leave.
Uniforms glister in a gathering rain.

'Thank you, sir. That's all.
And if you should remember something –'

This is no Incident Room, here, where spread clouds
Drive their load over obliterate ground:
Only a place drawn down into a past
Which will contain us all in dark solution.
Raindrops bounce and hover on the paving
In quick, unhealing rings; a sepia tree
Dries out behind our windy shawls of green.
A cold scent quickens in the formless air.

The Chestnut Tree

No Sandman, no soft-shoe shuffle
    About the garden,
Just light easing, the small quiver
    Of small creatures.

The shrine suffers a god's absence,
    Webbed and creviced:
A shell held to a green ear
    Where traffic hushes.

Dusk shakes out her pale children.
    Bits of life
Sidle across the cooling air,
    Smaller than angels.

The pond surfaces, the fish
    Nudge and wrinkle.
Another sunset works us down
    And down further.

We cannot name those four
    At the lawn's corners;
Night draws a hedge of fire
    Across our eyes.

The tall horse-chestnut sings
    About its dying:
Ring-marked, a house of knowledge
    Primed for the fall.

Next Door

The house empty next door,
   Snow a dullish blur
Caught between freeze and thaw –
   And emptier

That space pushed out from us
   Where the pulse faltered.
Absence, dust, terminus,
   And all altered.

Plates wiped into silence,
   Time beyond minding,
White on the garden fence,
   Clocks unwinding.

The daylight going, gone,
   Settled into night;
How strange our rooms have grown –
   Bubbles of light

Where conversations run
   From the walls we share,
The life, the voice, withdrawn
   Stripping us bare

With talk of pale china,
   Cold bits of iron,
Sticks of dark furniture,
   Scraps written on.

Caught between thaw and freeze,
   Snow breaks branches down
As it did, as it will,
   Eighty years flown.

The Candles

A candle at your window, Reagan told us,
Light it for Poland. Forty years ago
A Polish airman taught me his 'I love you',
Breaking strange language out for me like bread;
His red and silver lynx badged my small palm.
Salt on a childish tongue: under the stair
Our fat soap candles lay; they lit the climb
To bed, and winding-sheets as cold as wax.
Their black wicks lifted to an oily stain,
Then sirens howled the moon, the chopper came;
The barrage lifted, and we still had heads.

Now, the Advent Calendar counts down
Shutters of light on swiftly cooling earth,
And what is known becomes a blur of wind,
A stretch of grass, dressed with the death of leaves.
The candles for our tree are boxed and still,
They nuzzle blind, delaying their soft fuses,
And though white blossom and the red of blood
Are twisted hard against our expectation
We shall not light them for a blue Virgin,
Or for a country where the luck runs out.
We press against the echo of a word

And think of English trees, an All Saints' Night,
The mists taking the conifers apart,
The mortuary chapel shut, but the gates open
For congress of the living and the dead.
There are the candles, glimpsed and guttering,
Behind the iron curtains and the wall:
Slight fires upon a shelf of Polish graves
Whose marble crisps to angels, crucifixions,
Names cut from the roots of another tongue.
The letters dance in black, and under them
Crimsons and whites of silken immortelles.

The celebrants, the host of lesser lights,
An autumn Pentecost, a gift of tongues,
Flutter themselves away in cells of glass
Against the cities: Wilna, Warsaw, Cracow.
Their slim flames, fuelled by the airs we share,
Still say 'I love you' in the grass and chill.
Here the sad suitcase and the paper bag
Are finally unpacked; our shadows lean
Across this pale of loosening flesh and bone
Which knew, that for a space, candles would flower,
Whatever comes with night to put them out.